How to Pray for the Peace of Jerusalem:
A guide to praying for Israel, Jerusalem and God's Chosen People
Copyright 2013
Mike Evans

Published by TimeWorthy Books
PO Box 30000
Phoenix, AZ 85046-0009

Printed in the United States of America.

ISBN 0-935199-01-2

How to Pray for the Peace of JERUSALEM

A guide to praying for Israel, Jerusalem and God's Chosen People

MIKE EVANS

*Because the Sovereign LORD helps me I will
not be disgraced. Therefore I have set my face
like a stone, determined to do His will…
to pray for peace in Jerusalem.
May all who love this city prosper.*
Isaiah 50:7, Psalm 122:6 NLT

Jerusalem Prayer Team Members

There is no greater need today than to support Israel with our daily prayers. Israel is under attack on the political and military fronts and is threatened with total annihilation. But we believe in the power of prayer. This book is designed to help you to pray even more effectively for God's Chosen People.

When we pray for Jerusalem we are in obedience to the Great Commission. The Great Commission mandates that we be a witness unto Him in

Jerusalem, Judea and Samaria. Praying for the Peace of Jerusalem is sharing God's love and compassion.

I ask you to join me in prayer every day for Jerusalem and the nation of Israel. I pray that this booklet of prayers will be a help and an encouragement to you and that your life will be mightily blessed of God for your obedience!

Pray for the peace of Jerusalem: "May they prosper who love you. Peace be within your walls, Prosperity within your palaces." For the sake of my brethren and companions, I will now say, "Peace be within you" (Psalm 122:6-8).

This prayer was written by the Chief Rabbi of the state of Israel in 1948 and is prayed in synagogues the world over each Shabbat.

"Our Heavenly Father, Israel's Rock and Redeemer,
Bless the State of Israel, the first
flowering of our redemption.
Shield it under the wings of Your loving kindness
And spread over it the Tabernacle of Your peace.
Send Your light and truth to its leaders,
ministers and officials,
And direct them with good counsel before You."

"Strengthen the hands of the defenders
of our Holy land;
Grant them deliverance, our God,
And crown them with the crown of victory.
Grant peace in the land and everlasting
joy to its inhabitants."

"As for our brother, the whole house of Israel,
Remember them in all the lands of their dispersion,
And swiftly lead them upright to Zion your city,
And Jerusalem Your dwelling place,
As is written in the Torah of Moses Your servant:

HOW TO PRAY FOR THE PEACE OF JERUSALEM

*'Even if you are scattered to the furthermost
land under the heavens,
From there the Lord your God will
gather you and take you back.
The Lord your God will bring you to the land
Your ancestors possessed and you will possess it;
And He will make you more prosperous
and numerous than your ancestors.'"*
Deuteronomy 30:4-5

*"Unite our hearts to love and revere Your name
And observe all the words of Your Torah,
And swiftly send us Your righteous anointed
one of the house of David;
To redeem those who long for Your salvation."*

*"Appear in Your glorious majesty over
all the dwellers on earth,
And let all who breathe declare:
The Lord God of Israel is King
And His kingship has dominion over all.
Amen, Selah."*

Prayers for
JERUSALEM

"**L**ord God of Israel, Elohim, El Shaddai...we beseech you to keep watch over this Holy City. You have named it the Holy City of God where soon it shall be the place where Messiah Yeshua, Jesus Christ will establish His earthly throne and rule and reign as King of Kings and Lord of Lords over all the earth. Preserve and protect Your Chosen People who dwell there. Let those who curse Your name be brought down. Raise up all who faithfully call upon Your name for deliverance, health and prosperity, in Jesus' Name."

On that day, when all the nations of the earth are gathered against her, I will make Jerusalem an immovable rock for all the nations. All who try to move it will injure themselves... I will keep a watchful eye

over the house of Judah... Then the leaders of Judah will say in their hearts, 'The people of Jerusalem are strong, because the Lord Almighty is their God.'
Zechariah 12:3-5 (NIV)

"I pray for the leaders of Israel, President Shimon Peres, Prime Minister Benjamin Netanyahu and Nir Barkat the Mayor of this Holy City as well as the military leaders and officers. Protect and preserve them and give them wisdom from on High. Give them the strength and righteous indignation to not allow the dividing of the land! I pray for Christians the world over to recognize the unique position of Jerusalem in the Prophetic Promises of God for her end-time purposes."

The land shall not be sold for ever: for the land is mine; for ye are strangers and sojourners with me. **Leviticus 25:23**

"I pray, God, that You nullify the voices and speech of those who spew out lies and propaganda against Israel. I condemn every false doctrine and false religion that is set against God's Chosen People and the State of Israel, in Jesus' Name"

Deliver my soul. O Lord, from lying lips, and from a deceitful tongue. **Psalm 120:2**

Concise Prayers:

"**G**od of Israel, You have promised to establish the Holy City of Jerusalem. Today I pray that you will strengthen the hands of those who defend Jerusalem, and give them Your light to guide their way."

> *Nevertheless for David's sake did the LORD his God give him a lamp in Jerusalem, to set up his son after him, and to establish Jerusalem.* **1 Kings 15:4**

"Lord, You are the God of peace, and I ask today that Jerusalem will know Your peace. Though the enemies are gathered around the Holy City like vultures circling their prey, I ask that You deliver the City of David from their hands."

> *Pray for the peace of Jerusalem: they shall prosper that love thee.* **Psalm 122:6**

"Father in Heaven, we know that Your Son

loved Jerusalem. I pray today that You would shelter and shield the Holy City and her people from their enemies. Hide them like a chicken gathers her babies under her wings and keep them safe."

O Jerusalem, Jerusalem, thou that killest the prophets, and stonest them which are sent unto thee, how often would I have gathered thy children together, even as a hen gathereth her chickens under her wings, and ye would not! **Matthew 23:37**

"God of battles, You selected Jerusalem from all the cities of the earth as the place to establish Your name forever. You chose Your servant David as the leader and defender of Your people. Keep Your covenant with him today and arise to defend Jerusalem from destruction."

But I have chosen Jerusalem, that my name might be there; and have chosen David to be over my people Israel. **2 Chronicles 6:6**

"God of Zion, Your dwelling place in Jerusalem is under assault today. I ask that You would turn the hearts of the enemies of Your people to confusion and their plans to dust. Let Your Chosen People rejoice as they see Your deliverance, and let them learn Your truth and holiness."

Thus saith the LORD; I am returned unto

Zion, and will dwell in the midst of Jerusalem: and Jerusalem shall be called a city of truth; and the mountain of the LORD of hosts the holy mountain. **Zechariah 8:3**

"Lord, I pray today for the safety and security of the inhabitants of Jerusalem. Their enemies are many; their friends are few. Let me be a faithful friend to them. And I ask that for the sake of Your righteous Name You will defend and deliver them from evil."

In those days shall Judah be saved, and Jerusalem shall dwell safely: and this is the name wherewith she shall be called, The LORD our righteousness. **Jeremiah 33:16**

"Lord of Glory, as evil hearts devise wickedness against Your Holy City, I pray that You will cause their knees to bow before You. In the place where You have set Your Name, bring peace around Your throne. Even so come and bring peace to this earth."

At that time they shall call Jerusalem the throne of the LORD; and all the nations shall be gathered unto it, to the name of the LORD, to Jerusalem: neither shall they walk any more after the imagination of their evil heart. **Jeremiah 3:17**

"Lord, as You have delivered Your people time and again in the past, I pray that You would again arise for the defense of Jerusalem. Circle over the Holy City and hide her under the shadow of Your wings. Preserve and protect Israel today, Lord God."

As birds flying, so will the LORD of hosts defend Jerusalem; defending also he will deliver it; and passing over he will preserve it. **Isaiah 31:5**

"Lord, the beautiful city of Jerusalem is under attack today from every side. Defend Your Chosen People and their capital from political, military and economical threats and give victory to those who fight the evil forces arrayed against Jerusalem."

Beautiful for situation, the joy of the whole earth, is mount Zion, on the sides of the north, the city of the great King. **Psalm 48:2**

"God of Israel, today I ask that the city of Jerusalem see good from Your hand according to Your promises. We know that if You guard the city, the enemy will come against it in vain. So stand today upon the walls of Jerusalem, O Most High God."

The LORD shall bless thee out of Zion: and thou shalt see the good of Jerusalem all the days of thy life. **Psalm 128:5**

Prayers for Israel:

"**F**ather God, raise the hedge of protection high around all of Israel. Protect her from the satanic forces that are determined to destroy her and to discredit Your prophetic promises to her. Your Word is true, Oh Lord. As she stands on the brink of nuclear war, give great wisdom to her government and military leaders. Let the enemies of Israel see Your might and power demonstrated for the victory of Israel and let those who hate Israel be confounded."

> *O Lord, how many are my foes! How many rise up against me...But You are a shield around me, O Lord; You bestow glory on me and lift up my head.* **Psalm 3:1,3 (NIV)**

"I pray for the poor and impoverished living in Israel; the Holocaust survivors, the refuges from different lands retuning home to their land. May they bring with them a Divine supernatural power of the

7

Holy Spirit to all of Israel. Protect the families who are forced to live in bomb shelters from the deadly rockets of the enemy. Let them see Your hand of compassion and Divine protection upon them so they may rejoice in Your faithfulness."

The Lord is my rock, my fortress and my deliverer; my God is my rock, in Whom I take refuge, my shield and the horn of my salvation. He is my stronghold, my refuge and my savior—from violent men You save me. **II Samuel 22:2-3 (NIV)**

"God of Heaven and earth, protect the schools and the school children who are being targeted by enemy terrorists. Watch over the families who trust in Your name. Provide jobs and sufficient income for every family and reveal to them that it is by Your mercy and grace alone so they may come to believe in You, the One True God and Your Son Messiah Yeshua, in Jesus' Name!"

I will say of the Lord, 'He is my refuge and my fortress, my God, in Whom I trust.' Surely He will save you from the fowler's snare and from deadly pestilence. He will cover you with His feathers, and under His wings you will find refuge; His faithfulness will be your shield and rampart. You will not fear the terror of night, nor the arrow that flies by day. **Psalm 91:2-5 (NIV)**

Concise Prayers:

"**D**emonstrate Your grace and loving kindness to Your people so they will not forget that they are the apple of Your eye. Keep them under the shadow of your wings from those who persecute them "

You shall hide them in the secret place of Your Presence from the plots of man; You shall keep them secretly in a pavilion from the strife of tongues. **Psalm 31:20 (NKJV)**

"God, I ask You today to make me a witness for the defense of Zion. Let me know not rest or hold my peace. Keep strong within my heart a love for Jerusalem and Your Chosen People. Let me be part of their deliverance."

For Zion's sake will I not hold my peace, and for Jerusalem's sake I will not rest, until the righteousness thereof go forth as brightness, and the salvation thereof as a lamp that burns. **Isaiah 62:1**

"God of David, I pray that today You would arise and scatter the enemies of Israel and defend the city of Jerusalem. I know that one day You will rule the world from this sacred place, and I ask today that You will be the strength and shield of Zion."

And it shall be in that day, that living waters shall go out from Jerusalem; half of them toward the former sea, and half of them toward the hinder sea: in summer and in winter shall it be. And the LORD shall be king over all the earth. **Zechariah 14:8-9**

And many nations shall come, and say, Come, and let us go up to the mountain of the LORD, and to the house of the God of Jacob; and he will teach us of his ways, and we will walk in his paths: for the law shall go forth of Zion, and the word of the LORD from Jerusalem. **Micah 4:2**

"Lord of Israel, make me a watchman today for the Holy City and for the land of Israel. I pray that You would strengthen my resolve to stand for the Jewish people in private prayer and public support. Help me to sound the alarm so that others will join me in the defense of Zion."

I have set watchmen upon thy walls, O

Jerusalem, which shall never hold their peace day nor night: ye that make mention of the LORD, keep not silence. **Isaiah 62:6**

"Father I ask that today You would strengthen the defenses of Jerusalem. Do good to her people and rebuke those who would rise against her. We know that You are the true defense of Your Chosen People, and I pray Your strength be upon them".

Do good in thy good pleasure unto Zion: build thou the walls of Jerusalem.
Psalm 51:18

"Lord turn the Holy City to be a place of praise for Your Name. Cause those who would rise against Israel to stumble and break them into pieces. Establish Your purpose and guide those who stand upon the walls of Zion as ready servants to defend Israel."

To declare the name of the LORD in Zion, and his praise in Jerusalem. **Psalm 102:21**

"Lord of Your people, I cry out to you for the sake of Israel. I pray that You would gather and strengthen Your Chosen People as You have sworn in Your Word. Defend them against their enemies and make Your truth shine in their hearts."

The LORD doth build up Jerusalem: he

gathereth together the outcasts of Israel.
Psalm 147:2

"God, I cry out against the enemies of Israel today. I pray that their evil will turn upon them and consume them. I ask that Your hand be strong and mighty on behalf of the Jewish people and that You would give them Your victory and deliverance."

And in that day will I make Jerusalem a burdensome stone for all people: all that burden themselves with it shall be cut in pieces, though all the people of the earth be gathered together against it. **Zechariah 12:3**

"God of Power, I ask today that You strengthen the hands of those who defend Israel. Let the weakest among them be as mighty as Your servant David in battle. Let Your angels join the fight for the peace of Jerusalem and give victory over the forces of evil."

In that day shall the LORD defend the inhabitants of Jerusalem; and he that is feeble among them at that day shall be as David; and the house of David shall be as God, as the angel of the LORD before them. **Zechariah 12:8**

"Lord, no power of earth can stand against You.

Today I pray that You will display Your power on behalf of Your Chosen People. Deliver them from destruction and rain down Your righteous judgment on all who would come against Jerusalem"

And it shall come to pass in that day, that I will seek to destroy all the nations that come against Jerusalem. **Zechariah 12:9**

"Lord God, strengthen, settle and establish the Holy City and the Jewish people today. This sacred place is at the center of Your plans for our world. I come to Your throne today asking for Your mighty hand to work to defend Israel from those who would harm Your Chosen People."

Thus saith the Lord GOD; This is Jerusalem: I have set it in the midst of the nations and countries that are round about her. **Ezekiel 5:5**

Prayers of Intercession and Spiritual Warfare:

And I will give unto thee the keys of the kingdom of heaven: and whatsoever thou shalt bind on earth shall be bound in heaven; and whatsoever thou shalt loose on earth shall be loosed in heaven.
Matthew 16:19

"Father God, I know that the greatest spiritual battle is taking place right now over the Holy Land. Satan is once again trying to annihilate Your Chosen People and to discredit Your Word and Prophetic Promises to Israel. I come against this illegal warfare against Israel and her people, in Jesus' Name. I come against every deception and lie that is being propagated against them. I command the demonic powers of Satan be bound from this hideous action, in Jesus' name."

For we wrestle not against flesh and blood, but against principalities, against powers, against the rulers of the darkness of this world, against spiritual wickedness in high places. **Ephesians 6:12**

"I come against the lie that has many Christians deceived into believing that God is finished with Israel and has no further plans for her. This "Replacement Theology" is from the pit of hell! The Body of Christ has not replaced Your position, purpose and plans for Israel (Romans 11:1-2). Open the blind eyes of those who have accepted this deception in their hearts and reveal to them Your everlasting purposes for Israel, in Jesus' Name."

For there shall arise false Christs, and false prophets, and shall shew great signs and wonders; insomuch that, if it were possible, they shall deceive the very elect. **Matthew 24:24**

"I come against the propaganda and lies that are designed to make Israel appear as the terrorist aggressor and the Palestinians as the victims! Lord God, let the world see the lie the media is perpetuating and reveal the truth of the promises You gave to Israel as her land of inheritance."

Let the lying lips be put to silence; which speaks grievous things proudly and contemptuously against the righteous.
Psalm 31:18

"I come against the satanic anti-Semitic hatred that is being instilled into the minds of people in order to convince nation after nation not to stand with and come to the aid of Israel in this, her greatest time of need! I decree the favor and love of God to be demonstrated to her so the world may see and comprehend the mercy, love and power of the God of Abraham, Isaac and Jacob, in Jesus' Name!"

It is God that avengeth me, and that bringeth down the people under me. And that bringeth me forth from mine enemies: thou also hast lifted me up on high above them that rose up against me: thou hast delivered me from the violent man.
II Samuel 22:48-49

The **Spiritual Gift** of **Intercessory Prayer:**

I will pray with the spirit and I will pray with the understanding also: I will sing with the spirit, and I will sing with the understanding also. **I Corinthians 14:15**

If you have the gift of praying in the heavenly language, this is the most powerful form of intercessory prayer!

Let the high praises of God be in their mouth, and a two edged sword in their hand; to execute vengeance upon the heathen, and punishments upon the people; to bind their kings with chains, and their nobles with fetters of iron; to execute upon them the judgment written: this honour have all his saints. Praise Ye the Lord. Psalm 149:6-9

Prayers for the Jerusalem World Center:

Thou shalt also decree a thing, and it shall be established unto thee: and the light shall shine upon thy ways. **Job 22:28**

"Father, I believe that You have Divinely inspired our Israel Ambassador, Dr. Mike Evans, to obtain and establish this new facility in the heart of Jerusalem that will house the Jerusalem World Center. I decree that it will be an outstanding witness of Your Light and Salt of the earth to all Jews. I pray a Divine Blessing on the Mandate of Prayer that will flow from this Jerusalem Prayer Center as people from every nation on earth will come and focus on the deliverance and salvation of Israel, in Jesus' Name."

And this gospel of the kingdom shall be preached in all the world for a witness unto all nations; and then the end shall come. **Matthew 24:14**

"I pray, Father God, that You raise up intercessors within the Body of Christ the world over. Raise up and set in position those who are the watchmen on the walls of Jerusalem to pronounce and declare the calls to prayer for Jerusalem."

Praying always with all prayer and supplication in the Spirit, and watching thereunto with all perseverance and supplication for all saints. **Ephesians 6:18**

Prayers for the Jerusalem Christian Heritage Center & Museum:

"I decree a supernatural demonstration of Your Power and Presence as Jews visit the new Christian Zionist Heritage Center. May they sense the love and compassion Christians the world over have for them, their culture and their heritage. Let them recall Who has declared the state of Israel into existence, not a man but You Almighty God. Bring to their remembrance all the mighty miracles You have provided since the days of Moses. Help them to recognize Your faithful miracle power to protect and keep alive such a tiny nation that the world has resented and hated."

I will tell of the kindnesses of the Lord, the

deeds for which He is to be praised, according to all the Lord has done for us—yes, the many good things he has done for the house of Israel, according to His compassion and many kindnesses. **Isaiah 63:7 (NIV)**

"Let there be an out-flowing of provisioning to anyone who comes there for refuge and aid. Let these provisions be supernaturally multiplied to them, just at Jesus multiplied the five loaves and two fishes to the multitude in need, in Jesus' Name. I pray that You will comfort, heal and provide for the poor of Israel and especially the elderly survivors of the Holocaust."

Defend the cause of the weak and fatherless; maintain the rights of the poor and oppressed. Rescue the weak and needy; deliver them from the hand of the wicked. **Psalm 82:3-4 (NIV)**

Prayers for the Jerusalem Prayer Center

"Lord God of Israel, anoint this prayer center with the power and might of Your Holy Spirit. Place the gift of Discernment and Intercession on those who intercede for all of Israel. Consecrate those who have dedicated and set themselves apart for this great ministry of prayer. Enlarge the stakes of their tent with the supernatural gifts of the Holy Sprit for healing, deliverance, wisdom, knowledge, prophecy and the working of miracles."

Now there are differences of administrations, but the same Lord... diversities of operations but the same God which worketh all in all... the manifestation of the Spirit is given to every man to profit withal... the word of wisdom... the word

of knowledge… faith… gifts of healing… the working of miracles… prophecy… discerning of spirits… divers kinds of tongues … and interpretation.
I Corinthians 12:4-10

"Our Father, lend Your ear to the prayers of the Jerusalem Prayer partners as together we unite and agree with Your Word for the Prophetic Promises You have declared over Jerusalem and the nation of Israel. Let Peace come through the soon return of Your Son, Messiah Yeshua, Jesus Christ, who will rule and reign over all the earth from the City of God, the Holy City… Jerusalem, for all of eternity!"
The eyes of the lord are upon the righteous and his ears are open unto their cry…. The righteous cry, and the Lord heareth, and delivereth them out of all their troubles.
Psalm 34:15-17

Praise the Lord for These Prophetic Promises of God for Israel:

And in that day, saith the Lord, will I assemble her that halteth, and I will gather her that is driven out, and her that I have afflicted; and I will make her that halted a remnant, and her that was cast far off a strong nation: and the Lord shall reign over them in mount Zion from henceforth, even forever. Micah 4:6-7

All of Israel shall be saved (Romans 11:26-27)

Israel will continue to be a nation (Genesis 17:7-8)

The Davidic Kingdom will be restored to Israel (Ezekiel 37:24-25)

Israel's enemies will be removed (Psalm 33:8-12)

Messiah Jesus will rule and reign over all the earth from His throne in Jerusalem (Zechariah 14:1-9)

A new Temple will be built on Mount Zion (Ezekiel 43:6-7)

Messiah, Yeshua Jesus will bring world peace (Isaiah 2:4)

There will be worldwide celebration of the Feasts of Tabernacles (Succoth) (Zechariah 14:16-17)

> *And the ransomed of the Lord shall return, and come to Zion with songs and everlasting joy upon their heads: they shall obtain joy and gladness, and sorrow and sighing shall flee away.* **Isaiah 35:10**

> *And it shall be in that day, that living waters shall go out from Jerusalem; half of them toward the former sea and half of them toward the hinder sea: in summer and in winter shall it be. And the Lord shall be*

king over all the earth: in that day shall there be one Lord, and His name one. **Zechariah 14:8-9**

Selah…think on that!

Jerusalem
PRAYER TEAM

Dear Jerusalem Prayer Partners,

Be assured that God will honor your faithfulness to obey His Word and to pray for the peace of Jerusalem! Consider yourself as a Chosen One of God for this purpose and time in the History of Israel, Jerusalem and the Holy Land! We shall rejoice together in eternity when the Lord reveals to us the world-changing power our prayers have had!

Blessed be the Lord out of Zion, which dwelleth at Jerusalem. Praise ye the Lord. **Psalm 135:21**

Your ambassador to Jerusalem,

Dr. Michael Evans